W9-BVV-467

ISBN 1 85103 311 4
Originally published as *Wolfgang Amadeus Mozart Découverte des Musiciens* jointly by Editions Gallimard Jeunesse & Erato Disques.
© & ℗ 1998 by Editions Gallimard Jeunesse & Erato Disques.
This edition first published in the United Kingdom jointly by Moonlight Publishing Ltd, The King's Manor, East Hendred, Oxon OX12 8JY
& The Associated Board of the Royal Schools of Music (Publishing) Limited, 24 Portland Place, London W1B 1LU.
English text © & ℗ 2001 by Moonlight Publishing Ltd & The Associated Board of the Royal Schools of Music.
Printed in Italy by Editoriale Lloyd

JB Moz

Wolfgang Amadeus
MOZART
FIRST DISCOVERY – MUSIC

Written by Yann Walcker
Illustrated by Charlotte Voake
Narrated by Michael Cantwell

The scene is Salzburg in Austria at the foot of the mountains. As soon as the sun rises the city is filled with sounds: the bells in the church tower chime, the workman's hammer rings, the shopkeeper whistles and

Mozart's mother

A LITTLE NIGHT MUSIC, 1ST MOVEMENT, ALLEGRO
MUSICAL SLEIGH-RIDE BY LEOPOLD MOZART

up above the sheep join in with their bells. In the midst of all this hubbub a baby is fast asleep. His name? Wolfgang Amadeus Mozart!

GAME

When you are out for a walk, try to name each and every sound you can hear: the sound of aircraft, of cars, of animals, and even of the wind. The game is to find as many sounds as you can. You can play it with your friends. The first to find ten wins!

Mozart's father

During the long winter nights, little Wolfgang plays by the fireside with his pet dog, Pimpernell. His sister, Nannerl, prefers to practise on the harpsichord. One day she asks him if

he would like to have a go. Without a word, Wolfgang sits down at the instrument. Lo and behold, not only does he repeat everything his sister has just played without a mistake, but he also improvises on the tunes!

Wolfgang, his father and his sister

Wolfgang is such a good musician that he is invited to play for the emperor. He sets off for Vienna and knocks at the palace door. The emperor asks him to play a piece without looking at either the instrument or his

hands! To be quite sure, he covers the keyboard with a piece of cloth. Little Mozart plays without the slightest difficulty. What a triumph! The astounded emperor applauds him and gives him a gold watch.

WITH YOUR EYES CLOSED

You probably have an instrument at home – a xylophone, a drum, a recorder or a piano... Do you think you could play it with your eyes shut like Mozart? It is worth practising because it will certainly impress your friends!

Piano
Drum
Recorder
Xylophone

Mozart is now seven years old. His proud father wants to show him off to the whole world! At Christmastime they arrive in France at the Chateau of Versailles. The king is in a good mood and asks Mozart to be his guest on

MAKE UP A SONG

Many pieces of music are written for a special occasion: a birthday, a wedding, a church service... Why don't you try to write a song to celebrate your next big occasion. You could teach it to your family and then you could all sing it together to your guests.

condition that he plays after dinner. He plays so well that every note seems like a jewel. Everyone is deeply moved and the king exclaims: 'Bravo! You have made our Christmas! Long live Mozart!'

Mozart leaves France and heads for England. In London he is granted an audience at the royal court. Queen Charlotte, who has a beautiful

A SONG FOR TWO VOICES

Mozart accompanied the queen. Why don't you ask someone to accompany you in a song you particularly like?

singing voice, asks him to accompany her on the harpsichord. By the end of the song Mozart has made a big impression. The queen is so touched she gives him a reward he will not forget: a kiss!

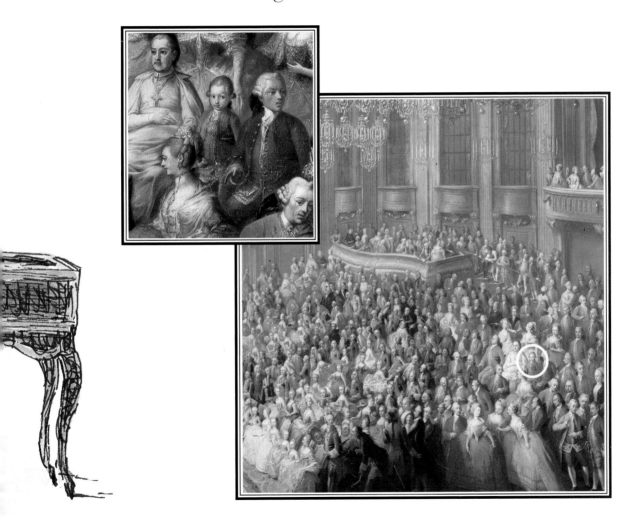

This time Mozart's travels take him to Italy. One day when he goes into the Sistine Chapel in Rome he hears church music. What a sweet sound: it seems to be coming from heaven! The beauty of the place overwhelms Mozart,

One of the frescos of the Sistine Chapel

IMAGINE

Music is often written to be played in a particular place. For example, some piano music is meant for the home, some trumpet music for the circus and some songs for church. Where do you think the next piece was meant to be played?

and he can't get it out of his mind. 'Now I too must write church music!'

Mozart is seventeen. He decides it's time to go back home to Salzburg. At last he will see his beautiful mountains again! What's more, he can portray in his music what he has seen and heard on his travels. It will certainly take some years for him to express all the impressions, feelings and recollections of the countries and events he has experienced.

WHAT ABOUT YOUR OWN TRAVELS?

Travel is very enriching, because different regions often have their own traditions, dances and style of dress. Music is frequently inspired by the climate or natural surroundings of a region: for example, Tyrolean songs recall the echoes of the mountains and Italian music seems to be brimming over with sun and joy and warmth. Can you remember a typical piece of music from a country or region you have visited?

Today

as in the past

Mozart's

music

is played

and loved.

THE TURKISH MARCH

Mozart wrote music for small groups of musicians. This type of music is called chamber music because it was meant to be played in quite small rooms – a drawing-room or even a bedroom. If instruments could be turned into people this music would be like a conversation between friends! Sometimes the piano is the only one to speak, as in *The Turkish March*. Sometimes the piano argues with the violins and cellos... It's quite simple: when there are two instruments playing, the piece is called a duet, when there are three, a trio. Four instruments play a quartet and five a quintet, as in the piece you are about to hear.

Is this a violin, a viola or a cello? The three instruments are the same shape. It is only their size that is different.

A string quartet is made up of two violins, a viola and a cello.

The inside of a piano is fascinating and very large in comparison with the keyboard.

TURKISH MARCH FROM SONATA IN A MAJOR, K. 331, 3RD MOVEMENT, ALLEGRETTO
HORN QUINTET IN E FLAT MAJOR, K. 407, 3RD MOVEMENT, RONDO-ALLEGRO

THE 'JUPITER' SYMPHONY

Mozart also wrote music for large groups of musicians, sometimes for over forty. These pieces could be either symphonies or concertos. In a symphony all the instruments are fully involved: strings, woodwind, brass and percussion. For instance, the first extract here is from the last movement of the 'Jupiter' Symphony. In a concerto, one instrument, the soloist, has a conversation with the orchestra. In the next extract you will hear a piano soloist.

The conductor beats the time with a baton in one hand and directs the different sections of the orchestra with the other hand.

Some conductors prefer not to use a baton and conduct with their bare hands.

SYMPHONY NO. 41 'JUPITER', 4TH MOVEMENT, MOLTO ALLEGRO
9 PIANO CONCERTO NO. 21, 2ND MOVEMENT, ANDANTE

THE MAGIC FLUTE

Mozart was passionate about opera. What is so wonderful about opera is not only can you listen to it but you can watch it as well: there are the costumes, the sets and the characters who sing. It's a bit like musical theatre. Through the singing Mozart makes us experience a whole range of human feelings: love, anger, joy and vengeance. For example, in *The Magic Flute*, which was Mozart's last opera, you can hear the Queen of the Night in a real rage.

This character is called Papageno. He is a bird-catcher and always wears a costume of bird feathers.

The character of the Queen of the Night requires the highest voice of all, called 'coloratura soprano'.

THE REQUIEM

In 1782 Mozart married his fiancée, Constanze. Mozart began to write a mass to celebrate their marriage. A mass set to music is like a sung prayer offered up to God. Listen to this passage from the Mass in C minor; you might well think you were listening to an angel sing. The last piece you will hear is from Mozart's Requiem, which is also the last piece Mozart wrote before he died in 1791. A requiem is a mass for the dead.

A sad song sung with feeling and reflection in a mass or requiem can be overwhelmingly powerful for those who are listening.

The sound of a large orchestra is impressively amplified in a church or cathedral.

MOONLIGHT PUBLISHING

Translator:
Penelope Stanley-Baker

ABRSM (PUBLISHING) LTD

Project manager:
Leslie East

Assisted by:
Susie Gosling

Text editor:
Lilija Zobens

Editorial supervision:
Caroline Perkins & Rosie Welch

Production:
Simon Mathews

English narration recording:
Ken Blair of BMP Recording

ERATO DISQUES

Artistic and Production Director:
Ysabelle Van Wersch-Cot

LIST OF ILLUSTRATIONS

KEY: **t** = top   **m** = middle   **b** = bottom
          r = right   **l** = left

PHOTOGRAPHIC ACKNOWLEDGEMENTS

Agostino Pacciani/Enguerand **20m**. Archiv für Kunst und Geschichte, Paris **6**, **7**, **10**, **15**, **16r**, **18**, **19**, **24t**, **26t**. Brigitte Enguerand **24m**. I. Derouville/Enguerand **22m**. Giraudon **9**. Marc Enguerand **24b**. Ph. Coqueux/Specto **26m**, **26b**. Photo Michel Szabo **22b**. Pierre-Marie Valat **11t**, **11bl**. Réunion des Musées Nationaux, Paris **12**. Scala **23**, **25**. Shimmel **20b**.

CD

I. It all begins in 1756
A Little Night Music,
1st movement, Allegro
Bournemouth Sinfonietta
Conducted by Theodor Guschlbauer
0630 11078 2
℗ Erato Classics SNC. Paris,
France 1973

Musical Sleigh-ride
by Leopold Mozart
Pro Arte Orchestra of Munich
Conducted by Kurt Redel
0630 14789 2
℗ Erato Classics SNC, Paris,
France 1972

2. A little genius on the harpsichord
Variations 'Ah vous dirai-je, maman'
Béatrice Martin, harpsichord
℗ Erato Disques S.A.. Paris,
France 1998

3. Famous at six
Sonata in C major, K. 6,
3rd movement, Minuet I
Georges Pludermacher. piano
0630 16244 2
℗ Erato Disques S.A.. Paris,
France 1996

4. At the French royal court
Concerto for Flute and Harp,
1st movement, Allegro
Lily Laskine, harp
Jean-Pierre Rampal. flute
Orchestre de Chambre
Jean-François Paillard
Conducted by Jean-François Paillard
4509 99651 2
℗ Erato Classics SNC. Paris,
France 1967

5. The Queen of England's kiss
The Magic Flute,
Duet 'Pa-pa-papagena'
Papageno. Hakan Hagegard
Papagena. Martina Bovét
Ensemble Orchestral de Paris

Conducted by Armin Jordan
4509 99654 2
℗ Erato Classics SNC. Paris.
France 1978

6. Thirteen already
'Coronation' Mass,
Sanctus
Lisbon Gulbenkian Foundation
Symphony Orchestra and Choir
Conducted by Theodor Guschlbauer
0630 10505 2
℗ Erato Classics SNC. Paris,
France 1978

7. When the Grand Tour is over
Don Giovanni,
Serenade
Don Giovanni. Ferruccio Furlanetto
Willi Rosenthal. mandoline
Berlin Philharmonic
Conducted by Daniel Barenboim
4509 94823 2
℗ Erato Disques S.A.. Paris.
France 1992
Coproduction Erato/RIAS Berlin
RIAS
BERLIN

8. Chamber music
Turkish March from Sonata in A major,
K. 331, 3rd movement, Allegretto
Alexei Lubimov. piano
2292 45619 2
℗ Erato Classics SNC. Paris,
France 1991

Horn Quintet in E flat major, K. 407,
3rd movement, Rondo-allegro
David Pyatt, horn
Kenneth Sillito, violin
Robert Smissen. Stephen Tees. violas
Stephen Orton. cello
0630 17074 2
℗ Erato Disques S.A.. Paris.
France 1997

9. Symphonic music
Symphony No. 41 'Jupiter',
4th movement, Molto allegro

Ensemble Orchestral de Paris
Conducted by Armin Jordan
0630 12813 2
℗ Erato Classics SNC, Paris,
France 1990

Piano Concerto No. 21,
2nd movement, Andante
Maria-João Pires. piano
Lisbon Gulbenkian Foundation
Chamber Orchestra
Conducted by Theodor Guschlbauer
4509 99653 2
℗ Erato Classics SNC. Paris.
France 1974

10. Opera
The Magic Flute,
Queen of the Night's aria
Queen of the Night. Sumi Jo
Ensemble Orchestral de Paris
Conducted by Armin Jordan
4509 99654 2
℗ Erato Classics SNC. Paris,
France 1978

II. Sacred music
Mass in C minor,
'Et incarnatus est'
Valerie Masterson. soprano
Lisbon Gulbenkian Foundation
Symphony Orchestra and Choir
Conducted by Michel Corboz
0630 14465 2
℗ Erato Classics SNC. Paris,
France 1978

Requiem,
Sanctus
Elly Ameling, soprano
Barbara Scheler. alto
Louis Devos. tenor
Roger Soyer. bass
Lisbon Gulbenkian Foundation
Symphony Orchestra and Choir
Conducted by Michel Corboz
4509 99652 2
℗ Erato Classics SNC. Paris,
France 1976

FIRST DISCOVERY - MUSIC

JOHANN SEBASTIAN BACH
LUDWIG VAN BEETHOVEN
HECTOR BERLIOZ
FRYDERYK CHOPIN
CLAUDE DEBUSSY
GEORGE FRIDERIC HANDEL
WOLFGANG AMADEUS MOZART
HENRY PURCELL
FRANZ SCHUBERT
ANTONIO VIVALDI